Piano · Vocal · Guitar

*Sarah McLachlan    Surfacing*

## CONTENTS

*Front Cover and Last Dance Photos by Dennis Keeley; Title page photo by Mark Van S;
Design and Illustrations by John Rummen*

ISBN 0-7935-8639-9

HAL•LEONARD®
CORPORATION
7777 W. BLUEMOUND RD. P.O. BOX 13819 MILWAUKEE, WI 53213

Visit Hal Leonard Online at
**www.halleonard.com**

# Building A Mystery

Words and Music by SARAH McLACHLAN
and PIERRE MARCHAND

Guitar 1: Capo VII
Guitar 2: Capo II

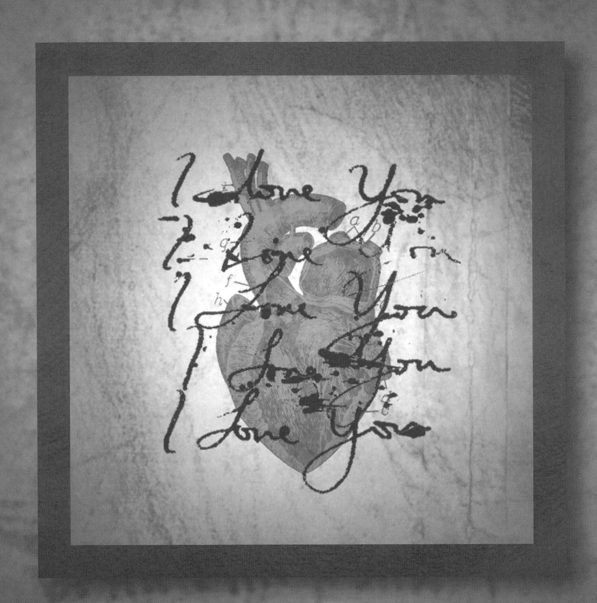

# I Love You

Words and Music by
SARAH McLACHLAN

Guitar: Capo I

**Slowly**

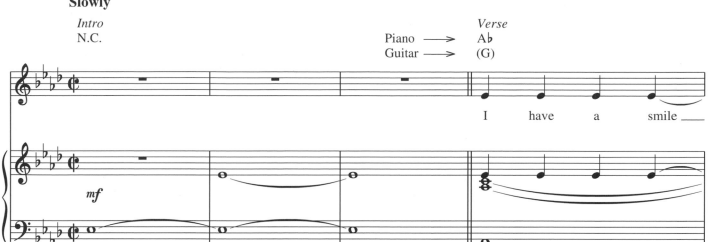

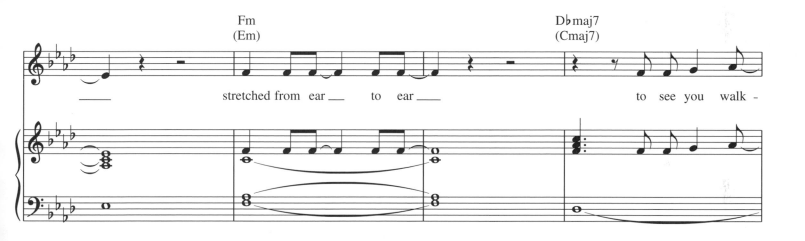

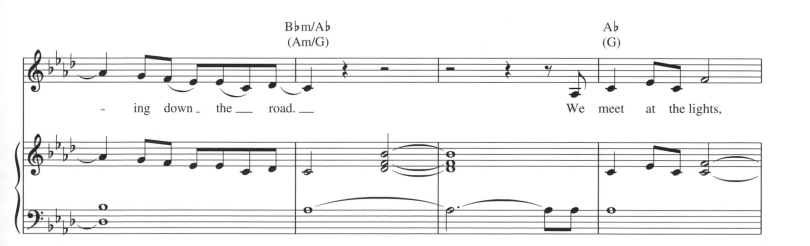

# Sweet Surrender

Words and Music by
SARAH McLACHLAN

you all the beauty you get

ou'd only let yourself believe

hat we are born innocent

ou'd                                        believe

hat                                          nt

me

it's easy we all falter

it's easy let it go...

it's easy let it go...

# Adia

Words and Music by SARAH McLACHLAN
and PIERRE MARCHAND

Guitar: Capo III

we all fal - ter.

And does it mat -

- ter? —

- ter? —

*Interlude*

# Do what you have to do

Words and Music by SARAH McLACHLAN
and COLLEEN WOLSTENHOLME

... (also called ... glass and object ...) for the formation of an image of the object under observation, and an *eyepiece* for magnifying the image. These parts are set in ...

PRINCIPLE OF THE TELESCOPE.
Explanation appears in text.

... tube so constructed that the observer can ... lengthen or shorten the distance between them. Astronomical telescopes are of two types, re-... fracting and reflecting. In refractors the ob-...

# Witness

Words and Music by SARAH McLACHLAN
and PIERRE MARCHAND

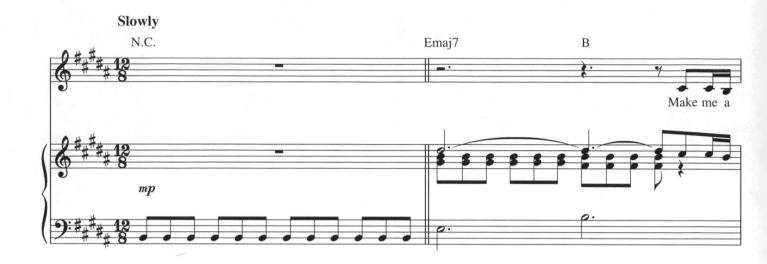

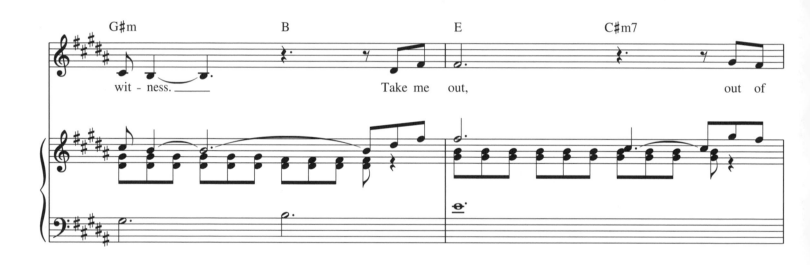

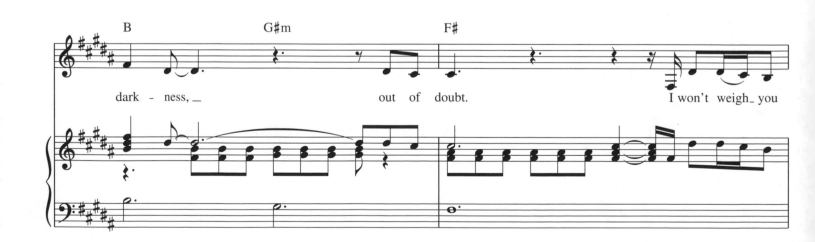

change come _____ while we're wait-ing?

Ev-'ry-one is

wait - ing.

wait - ing.

Solo ends

Will we

wait - ing. _

# Angel

Words and Music by
SARAH McLACHLAN

*Original key: Db Major. This edition has been transposed down one half-step to be more playable.*

# Black & White

Words and Music by
SARAH McLACHLAN

**Moderately**

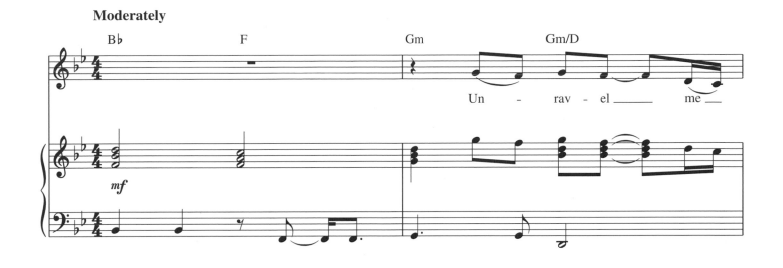

Un - rav - el ____ me ____

a dis - tant chord. ____ On the out - side is ____ for - got -

ten, ____ a con - stant ____ need ____ to get a - long ____ and the an -

# Full of Grace

Words and Music by
SARAH McLACHLAN

**Gently**

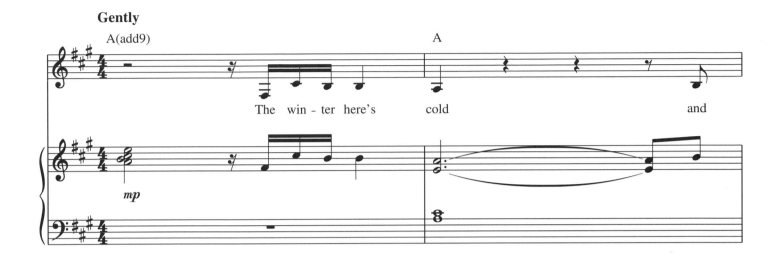

The win-ter here's cold and

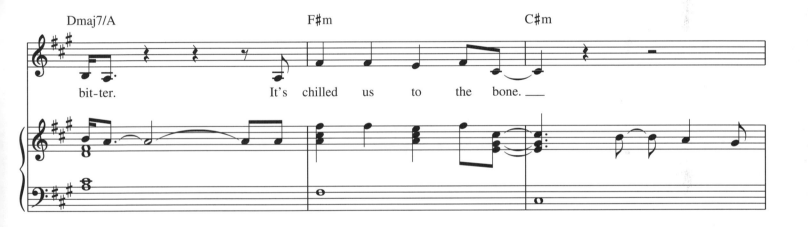

bit-ter. It's chilled us to the bone.

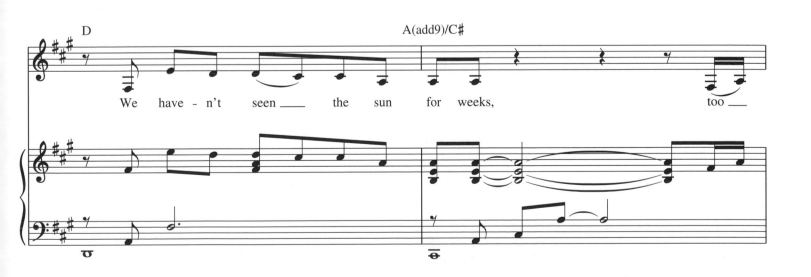

We have-n't seen ___ the sun for weeks, too ___

# Last Dance

Music by
SARAH McLACHLAN

# Building A Mystery
## (Guitar Part)

Words and Music by
SARAH McLACHLAN and
PIERRE MARCHAND

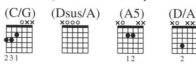

(C/G)  (Dsus/A)  (A5)  (D/A)

**Gtr. 1 Tuning, Capo VII:**
① = D  ④ = D
② = A  ⑤ = A
③ = G  ⑥ = E

**Gtr. 2 Tuning, Capo II:**
① = D  ④ = D
② = B  ⑤ = A
③ = G  ⑥ = E

**Gtr. 3 Tuning:**
① = D  ④ = D
② = B  ⑤ = A
③ = G  ⑥ = E

**Intro**

**Relaxed**

* Gtr. 1 chord symbols
** Gtr. 2 chord symbols

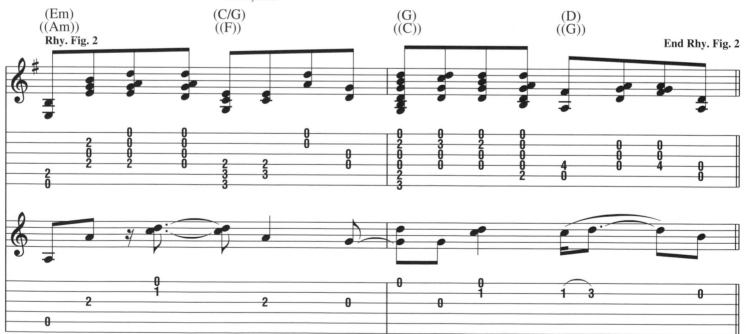

**Verse**

**Guitar Solo**

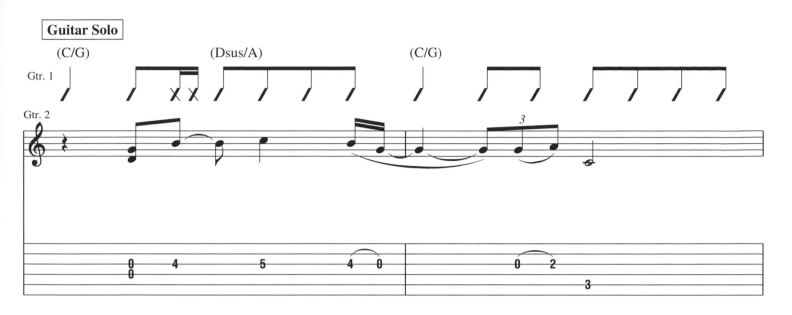

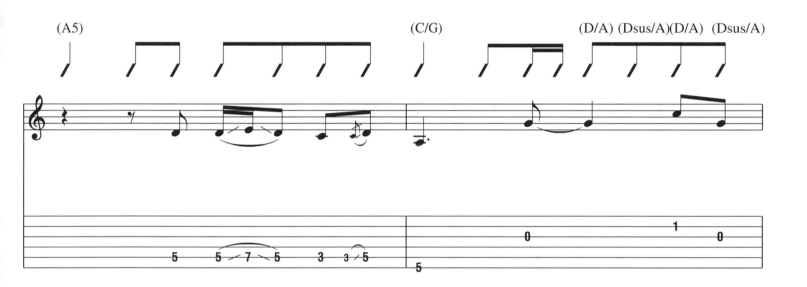

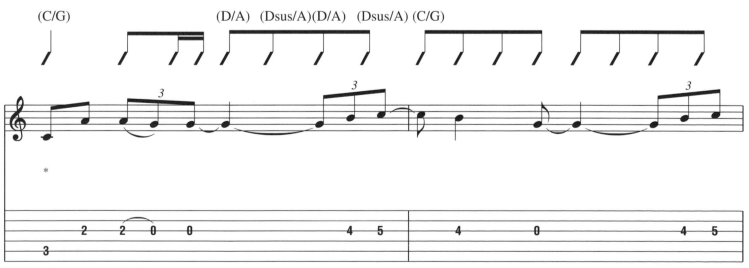

\* Reverse gtr. arr. for Gtr. 2.

**Outro-Chorus**

# I Love You
## (Guitar Part)

Words and Music by
SARAH McLACHLAN

Gtr. 1: Capo I

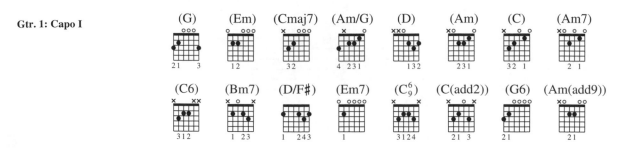

**Sample Strum Pattern**

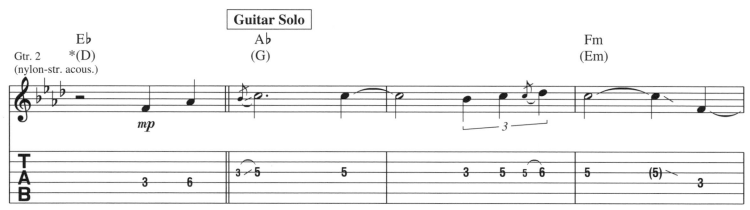

\* Symbols in parentheses represent chord names respective to capoed guitar.
Symbols above reflect actual sounding chord.

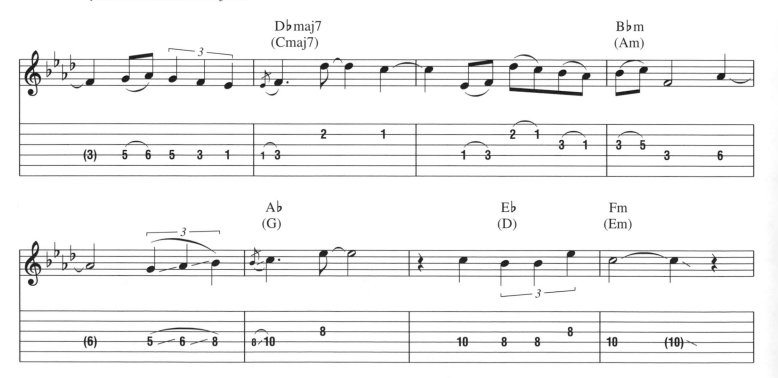

**Outro-Guitar Solo**

*Begin Fade*

*Fade Out*

# Sweet Surrender

## (Guitar Part)

Words and Music by
SARAH McLACHLAN

**Verse**

Gtr. 2: w/ Rhy. Fig. 1, 2 times, simile
Gtr. 1 tacet

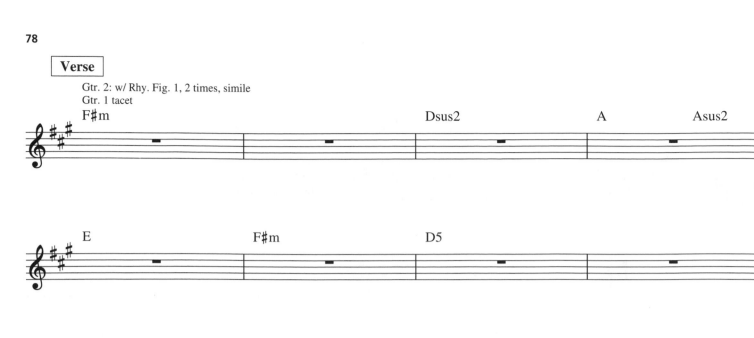

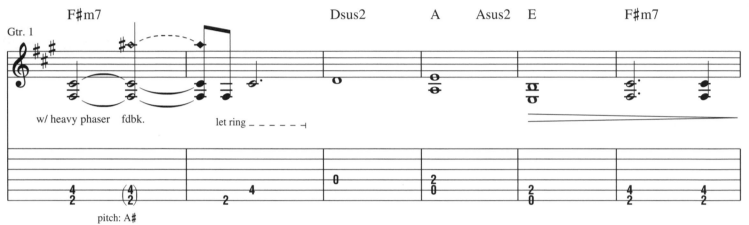

Gtr. 1 tacet    Gtr. 2: w/ Rhy. Fig. 2, simile

**Chorus**

Gtr. 2: w/ Rhy. Fig. 3

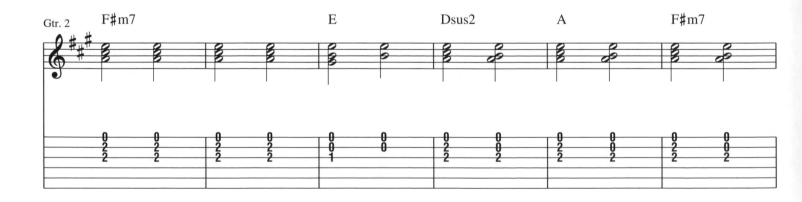

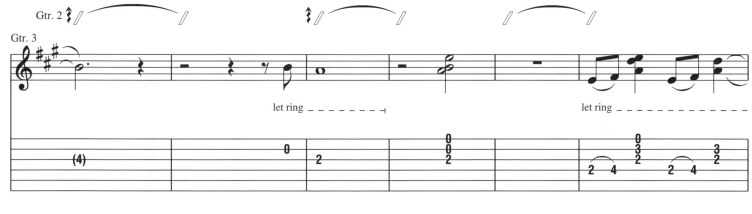

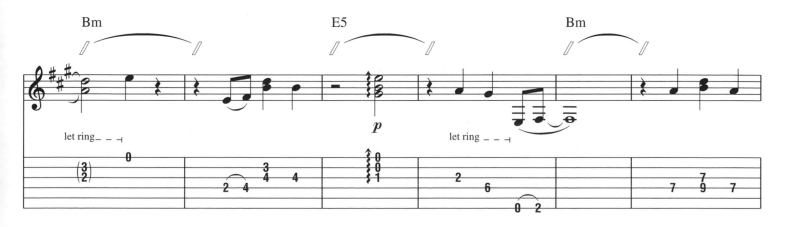

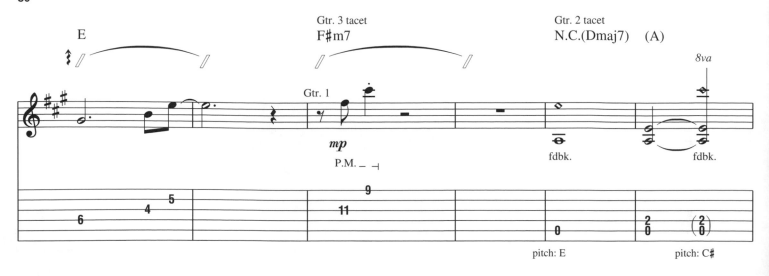

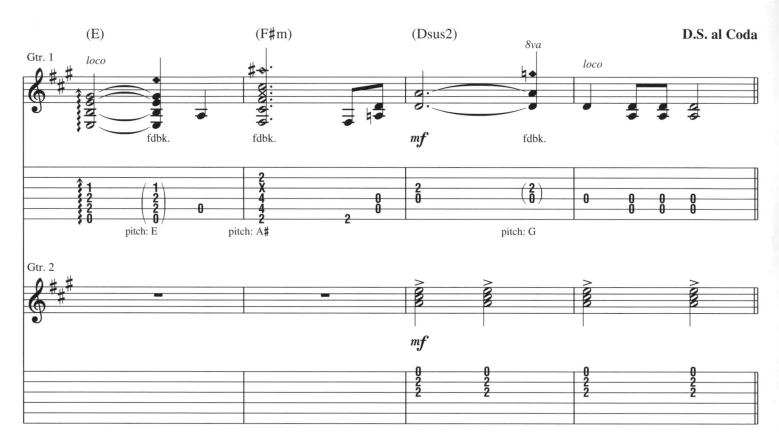

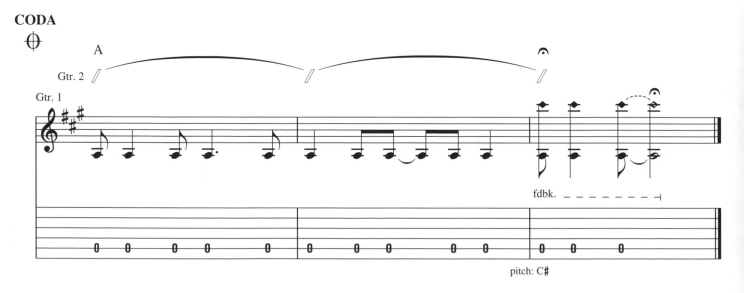

# Adia

## (Guitar Part)

Words and Music by
SARAH McLACHLAN and
PIERRE MARCHAND

82

# Witness

## (Guitar Part)

Words and Music by
SARAH McLACHLAN and
PIERRE MARCHAND

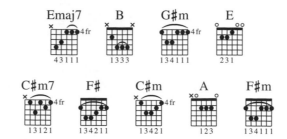

**Sample Strum Pattern**

**Guitar Solo**

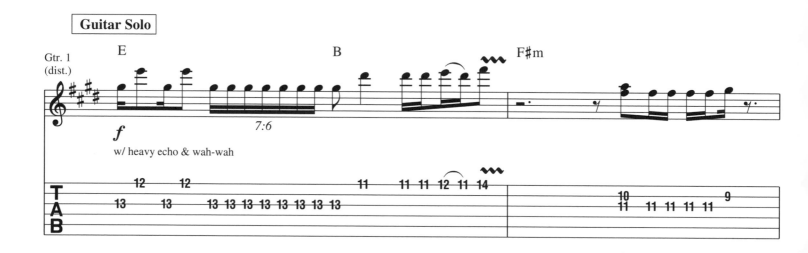

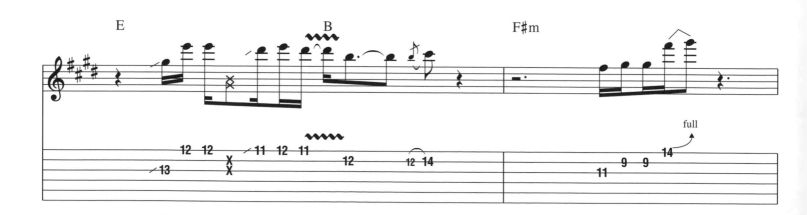

\* Played behind the beat.

# Do what you have to do

## (Guitar Part)

Words and Music by
SARAH McLACHLAN and
COLLEEN WOLSTENHOLME

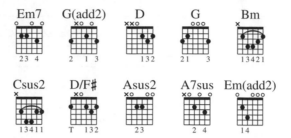

**Sample Strum Pattern**

# Angel

## (Guitar Part)

Words and Music by
SARAH McLACHLAN

\* **Capo I**

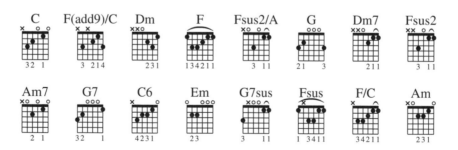

**Sample Strum Pattern**

\* to match recording

# Black & White
## (Guitar Part)

Words and Music by
SARAH McLACHLAN

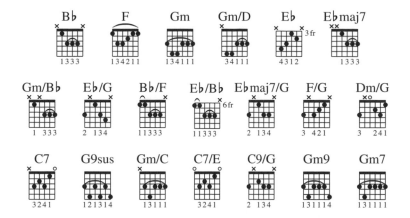

**Sample Strum Pattern**

# Full of Grace
## (Guitar Part)

Words and Music by
SARAH McLACHLAN

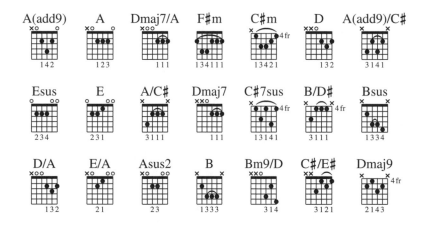

**Sample Strum Pattern**

# Last Dance

## (Guitar Part)

Music by
SARAH McLACHLAN

**\* (Tune Down 1/4 Step)**

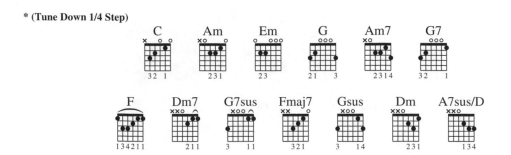

## Sample Strum Pattern

\* to match recording